Ancient Myths
Jason and the
Argonauts

Created and designed by
David Salariya

Written by
John Malam

Illustrated by
David Antram

Sandy Creek
NEW YORK

An Imprint of Sterling Publishing
387 Park Avenue South
New York, NY 10016

Series creator: David Salariya
Author: John Malam
Editors: Michael Ford, Nadia Higgins
Illustrations: David Antram

ISBN 978-1-4351-5122-2

Manufactured in Heyuan Guangdong Province, China
Lot #:
2 4 6 8 10 9 7 5 3 1
06/13

Jason and the Argonauts

Table of Contents

The World of Ancient Mythology

The ancient Greek civilization was one of the greatest the world has witnessed. It spanned nearly 2,000 years, until it was eventually overwhelmed by the Roman Empire in the second century B.C. At its height, the ancient Greek world extended far beyond what we know as modern Greece.

We owe much to the ancient Greeks. They were great scientists, mathematicians, writers, and thinkers. They were also brilliant storytellers. Many of the tales they told were in the form of poems, often thousands of lines long. The Greeks wrote poems on many kinds of human experiences, such as love, friendship, war, revenge, and history. The most famous of the poems that have passed down to us are epic tales of courage and warfare, where gods, heroes, and monsters struggle against great odds.

A map showing the ancient Greek mainland, surrounding islands, and neighboring lands

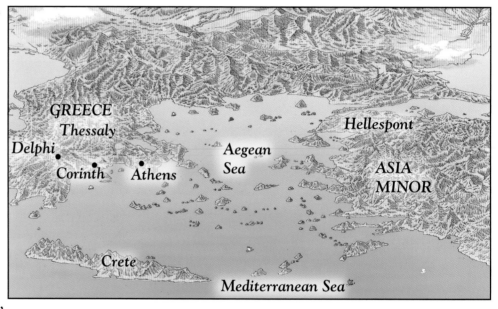

What is incredible is that until the eighth century B.C., the Greeks had no recognized form of writing. All of their stories, lengthy as they were, were handed down from generation to generation by word of mouth. The people who told them were often professional storytellers who performed in towns throughout the Greek world. They were called "rhapsodes," which means "song-stitchers." As a rhapsode spoke or sang the words of his story, he stitched its many twists and turns together. Often several versions of the same myth existed, depending on who told it and when. What follows is one version of Jason and the Argonauts.

If you need help with any of the names, go to the pronunciation guide on page 31.

Meet the Storyteller

Greetings citizens. Gather round. I am the rhapsode—the teller of stories. My tale is about a boy, born to be king, whose birthright was cruelly taken from him. His name was Jason, and his future lay across dangerous seas in the faraway land of Colchis. There he would find the fabulous Golden Fleece, the dazzling skin of a flying, talking ram. His mission was to seize the fleece and return with it. If he was successful, he would be made king. However, once Jason's ship was out of sight, no one thought they would ever see him alive again. Lend me your ears, for ...

I come this day from far away
With a tale to tell that spins a spell,
Which you will hear—if you draw near—
Of times of old and heroes bold.

So gather round and hear my story,
Which I will weave from ancient glory
By joining threads from start to end
That you may pass on to a friend.

There Was a Boy Named Jason

My story begins in a town in Greece called Iolcus. It lay on the coast of the Aegean Sea, in the kingdom of Thessaly. Iolcus had been founded by King Cretheus. He promised that when he died, his son Aeson would inherit the throne and become the next king.

Cretheus had another son, Pelias, who was Aeson's younger half-brother. Unknown to Aeson, Pelias wanted to be the next king. When their father died, Pelias seized his chance and declared himself the new ruler of Iolcus. Fearing he might be surrounded by enemies, Pelias consulted an oracle who predicted his future. Pelias learned that he would be punished for stealing the throne of Iolcus: One day he would be killed by a descendant of the royal family. Cruel Pelias tried to change the future. He murdered almost all of his relatives in the royal family so they wouldn't come after him. Last of all, Pelias went after the son of Aeson and Alcimede—a baby boy named Jason.

Oracles told the future

The Greeks asked oracles to predict their futures so they could prepare themselves for what was to come. It was believed that oracles revealed the gods' messages on Earth. A pilgrim such as Pelias visited an oracle and asked a question. The pilgrim believed the oracle's answer came from a god.

The name Pelias

When Pelias was a baby, a horse kicked him in the face. He was left with a purple mark on his cheek. This mark was known as a "pelion," and he was named Pelias because of it.

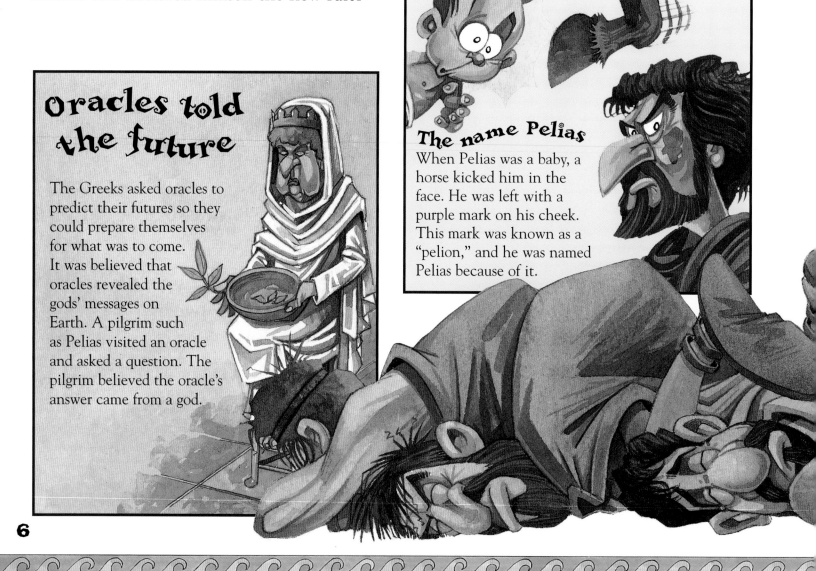

Raised by a Centaur

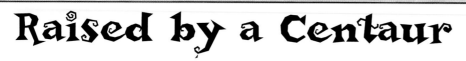

A mother's duty is to protect her child, and that is what Alcimede did. She pretended her baby was already dead, but really he was only sleeping. When Pelias came to kill Jason, he saw Alcimede and other women standing over the baby's still body. They were crying, beating their chests, and pulling their hair as if to mourn the baby. Pelias was fooled. He let Alcimede take Jason away from Iolcus to bury the boy's body, as was the custom.

Alcimede took Jason to Mount Pelion, the tallest mountain in Thessaly, and left him in the care of Chiron the centaur. Chiron was not like other centaurs. His front legs were like those of a human, not those of a horse. Chiron also was wise and kind. He raised Jason, feeding him on meat from rabbits and teaching him all he knew. He taught him medicine, and this knowledge gave the boy the name by which some know him—Jason the Healer.

Centaurs

In the forests and mountains of northern Greece lived the centaurs. They were wild and uncontrollable flesh-eating monsters, part horse, part human. They liked the taste of alcohol, which sent them into a drunken rage. Centaurs fought their enemies with tree stumps and boulders.

Ask the storyteller

Did Chiron tell Jason what Pelias had done?

When Jason was old enough to understand, Chiron told him he was the son of Aeson and that Pelias had stolen the throne of Iolcus. From then on, Jason was determined to remove Pelias from power.

Jason Sets Off to Iolcus

There came a time when Jason knew he must leave the safety of his mountain home. He was young and strong, and his heart ruled his head. He had been taught to respect those older and wiser than he, but there was one elder for whom he felt only hatred—Pelias, his uncle and unlawful king. Jason longed for Pelias's downfall.

On the way to Iolcus, Jason met an ugly old woman. She was stranded on the bank of the River Anaurus, unable to cross its rushing water. Passersby refused to take pity on her. Only Jason stopped to help. Unknown to Jason, the old woman was the goddess Hera in disguise. She too wanted Pelias punished, for he had offended her by not making sacrifices in her name. From now on, Hera would protect Jason at all times.

Jason meets Pelias

As Jason carried the old woman across the river, he stumbled and lost a sandal. Meanwhile, an oracle had warned Pelias to beware of a one-sandaled man. One day, as Pelias was sacrificing a lamb, he saw a tall youth wearing only one sandal. Remembering the oracle's words, Pelias asked his name. The youth replied he was Jason, son of Aeson.

I've lost my sandal!

11

I've lost my sandal!

Ask the storyteller

Did Jason know he was talking to Pelias?

At first, Jason did not know the name of the man with the lamb. Sensing this, Pelias had time to plan how to rid himself of Jason.

11

Jason Is Sent on a Mission

Pelias thought he knew the perfect way to get rid of Jason. He asked Jason what he would do if an oracle had given him a prophecy about a dangerous stranger. Of course, Pelias was really thinking of the oracle's warning to himself. It was a trap, which Jason did not see, for he still had no idea that the man was Pelias.

Jason thought for a while and then gave his answer. He told Pelias he would send the stranger to fetch the Golden Fleece from Colchis—but the words Jason spoke were not his! The goddess Hera had put them into his mouth as part of her plan to punish Pelias.

Only then did Pelias reveal who he was. As anger swelled in his heart, Jason told Pelias that he had come to take back the throne of Iolcus. Crafty Pelias said he could have it—in exchange for the Golden Fleece. It would be a dangerous mission for a mortal, and Pelias expected Jason to die.

Fetch me the Golden Fleece!

Jason will work for me, and I will protect him!

Oh Hera! What have I said?

The Golden Fleece

The Golden Fleece was the shimmering skin of the talking ram Chrysomallus. This winged creature had rescued two children and flown them to Colchis. Here, the ram was sacrificed in thanks to the gods. Its fleece was hung from a tree, guarded by a serpent that never slept.

GREECE

Iolcus

Euxine Sea

Colchis

Ask the storyteller

Where was Colchis?

Colchis was far away from Greece, at the eastern end of the Black Sea, which the Greeks called the Euxine Sea. It was in a remote area surrounded by mountains.

The Argonauts Are Assembled

Showing no fear, Jason accepted the challenge that Pelias had put to him. To cross the sea to Colchis, Jason needed a magnificent ship. He asked a craftsman called Argus to build one with timber from the forests of Mount Pelion, Jason's childhood home. The vessel was to be fitted with oars for a crew of 50 men.

Skilled though he was, Argus could not complete the task alone. The goddess Athena came to his aid. She gave the ship a figurehead cut from an oak tree sacred to the great god Zeus. The figurehead had the power of speech and would guide Jason on his mission.

The ship was named *Argo*, in honor of Argus. It was a fitting name, for it meant "swift." Jason called for a crew, and 50 men volunteered to sail with him. They are the heroes of this story and are known as the Argonauts—the men who sailed in the *Argo*. At dawn, the *Argo* headed east for Colchis.

Women of Lemnos

The *Argo* stopped first at the island of Lemnos. Only women lived there, as they had killed their menfolk and taken their weapons. Some Argonauts fell in love with the women and wanted to stay, but the hero Hercules convinced them to come back to the *Argo*.

Welcome, fellow Argonaut!

Ask the storyteller

What did the soothsayer predict?

One of the Argonauts was Idmon, a soothsayer. He told Jason the voyage would end well, but that he, Idmon, would not live. Despite predicting his own death, Idmon still joined the mission.

Jason Kills King Cyzicus

The *Argo* continued her voyage across the blue Aegean Sea, sailed through the Hellespont, the narrow strait that separates Europe from Asia, and entered the Sea of Marmara. She sailed to the city of Cyzicus, where the Argonauts were warmly welcomed. King Cyzicus invited the men to join him at his wedding feast. The Argonauts filled their bellies with food and wine. Then, anxious not to overstay their welcome, they said goodbye to their hosts. Little did they know that a tragedy was about to befall them all.

The Argonauts set sail into the night. Barely had the crew rowed the *Argo* out of sight when a storm blew the ship back to Cyzicus. Thinking the Argonauts were pirates, soldiers from Cyzicus attacked them in the darkness. Men who had shared food together as friends fought as enemies. In the confusion, Jason drove his spear through King Cyzicus!

Hercules is lost

After the tragedy, the *Argo* sailed on. Hercules, the strongest Argonaut, challenged the others to a rowing contest. One by one, the exhausted men dropped out, until Jason fainted and Hercules broke his oar. When the ship came to rest on the banks of a river, Hercules went in search of a tree from which to make a new oar. The next morning, Jason sailed on without Hercules. This hero took no further part in the quest for the Golden Fleece.

Ask the storyteller

What happened to Hercules?

Hercules, the greatest of all Greek heroes, went on to have his own adventures. He was set a series of tasks, which became known as the Twelve Labors of Hercules. His first labor was to kill the Nemean Lion, which he did with his bare hands.

The Blind Man and the Harpies

The *Argo* arrived at Salmydessus. This place was near the Bosporus Channel, which joined the Sea of Marmara to the Black Sea. Here lived Phineus, a king with the gift of seeing the future. Yet the gods could take gifts as well as give them, and they had taken Phineus's eyes. From then on, he could see the future, but not the present. This was not all. Poor Phineus was also plagued by two harpies who stole food from his table and left him forever hungry.

Jason asked Phineus what he must do to capture the Golden Fleece. Phineus promised to help if Jason rid him of the harpies. A feast was laid, and the Argonauts waited for the greedy demons to arrive. Luckily, two of the Argonauts, Calais and Zetes, happened to have wings. When the harpies swooped down, Calais and Zetes flew at them with swords. The harpies fled in fear. Free from the monsters, Phineus could finally eat in peace. In return, he warned Jason about a danger that lay ahead.

Body-snatching harpies

The harpies, whose name means "snatchers," were the winged women Aello ("Storm") and Ocypete ("Swift Flier"). They were known for swooping down and snatching children who were never to be seen again.

Ask the storyteller

Where did the harpies go?

After leaving Phineus alone, the harpies flew off to start a new life on the island of Crete.

19

At the Clashing Rocks

The danger that Phineus told Jason about stood in wait at the approach to the Bosporus Channel. Here were the Clashing Rocks—two towers of rock that guarded the narrow strait like soldiers. The menacing rocks destroyed all who tried to pass between them, moving toward each other until the unfortunate ship was crushed to splinters.

Jason had no choice. If he wanted to sail across the Black Sea and on to Colchis, he had to find a way past the Clashing Rocks. Phineus had told him what to do. Jason released a dove, and as it flew between the rocks, the mighty towers shook and crashed together, nipping only a feather from the bird's tail. Just as Phineus had predicted, the rocks then moved back to their waiting positions, giving the *Argo* the chance to slip through the channel unharmed.

Orpheus, the singing poet

As the *Argo* passed safely through the Bosporus Channel, Orpheus sang and played his lyre to calm the other Argonauts. His singing was so sweet it could tame even wild beasts.

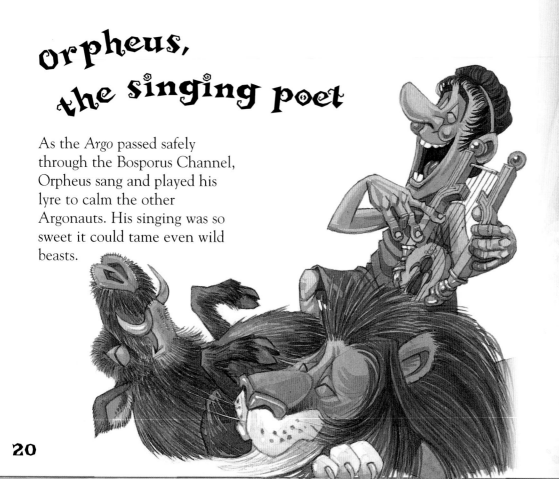

Phew! That was close!

Ask the storyteller

What happened to the rocks?

The Clashing Rocks' ship-crushing days ended when they failed to trap the *Argo*. From that day on, they never moved again, and sailors were no longer afraid of them.

Jason Reaches Colchis

At the far end of the Black Sea, Jason and the Argonauts reached Colchis. All thoughts turned toward taking the Golden Fleece from Aeetes, the ruthless king who owned it. Aeetes promised the fleece to Jason on the condition that Jason complete three tasks: plough a field using fire-breathing bulls; sow the field with teeth from the Dragon of Cadmus; and kill the skeleton warriors who grew from the teeth and burst through the soil.

Unknown to Aeetes, the goddess Hera had made Medea, his daughter, fall in love with Jason. It was all part of Hera's plan to destroy Pelias. Medea gave Jason a potion that made him invincible for a day, which allowed him to complete the difficult tasks. In return for Medea's help, Jason promised to marry her, as long as she returned to Greece with him.

The Dragon of Cadmus

This monster, whose eyes flashed fire and whose body was filled with poison, had been slain by the hero Cadmus. The dragon's magical teeth were then pulled out and shared between Cadmus and King Aeetes of Colchis. When sown in the ground, skeleton warriors came forth.

Ask the storyteller

How did Jason kill the skeleton warriors?

Medea told Jason to throw a boulder among them. This would confuse the warriors and make them think they were being attacked by each other. As they fought themselves, Jason easily cut them down one by one.

Jason Takes the Golden Fleece

Did you really think King Aeetes would hand over the Golden Fleece? Aeetes wanted the golden treasure to stay hanging in the oak tree, guarded by the sleepless serpent. He never expected Jason to complete the tasks he'd set for him, but neither did he imagine his daughter would work against him!

Once again, Medea, whose name means both "cunning" and "knowing," helped Jason. At night, she led him to the sacred grove of the Golden Fleece. Even in the darkness, its wool sparkled. Medea cast a spell over the fleece's fork-tongued guardian. Then she placed magic drops into its eyes, which made the great snake slump to the ground fast asleep. Quickly, Jason snatched the fleece and returned to the *Argo* with Medea.

Sleep, serpent, sleep.

Aeetes gives chase

As the new day dawned, King Aeetes discovered he had lost not one, but his two most precious treasures in life—the Golden Fleece *and* his daughter. He sent a fleet of fast ships to chase after the *Argo*, but even he could not imagine what cunning Medea would do next.

He's got the Golden Fleece!

ZZZZZZZ

Ask the storyteller

What did Medea do next?

The goddess Hera made Medea do a wicked thing. Medea took her brother Apsyrtus hostage. She killed him, chopped up his body, and threw the pieces into the sea. When her father's ships stopped to collect the pieces, the *Argo* sailed away.

Song of the Sirens

The voyage home was as difficult as the journey to Colchis had been. Blown far off course, the *Argo* sailed to the coast of Italy, until she came to the island of Anthemoessa, which means "flowery." On this island lived three sirens, demons of the sea with bodies of birds and heads of women. Their beautiful singing was a sound all sailors feared because it enchanted men and lured their ships to crash onto the rocks.

This was a fate the *Argo* avoided. Jason commanded Orpheus to sing for the Argonauts. As the crew listened to their companion's sweet voice, they rowed the ship to safety. Only one sailor, Butes, was lured by the song of the sirens. He jumped into the water and swam to them.

Ask the storyteller

Did Jason marry Medea?

Yes, he did. They were married on the island of Corfu, where they spent their wedding night in a cave, sleeping on the Golden Fleece.

Washed ashore

From Corfu, a tidal wave swept the *Argo* south, onto the deserts of northern Africa. For nine days, the Argonauts carried their ship on their backs, until they reached the Mediterranean Sea and set sail once more.

Sing louder, Orpheus!

Let my song fill your ears. It will take away your fears.

Talos the giant

I'm leaking to death!

The Argonauts reached the island of Crete. Here they met Talos, a giant with a bronze body. He pelted them with rocks, until Medea cast a spell to make him pull a plug from his ankle. Out poured his liquid metal "blood," and his life drained away.

27

The End of the Story

Jason, Medea, and the Argonauts finally reached Iolcus. King Pelias never dreamed that Jason would return, convinced that the mission to take the Golden Fleece was an impossible one. While Jason had been away, Pelias had killed Aeson and Alcimede, Jason's parents. Now the time had come for this evil man, stealer of the throne of Iolcus, destroyer of the royal family, to die—but not by the hand of Jason.

For one last time, Medea used her cunning. As before, the goddess Hera willed her on in order to punish Pelias. Medea said she could make new life from old. As proof, she killed an old ram and put its pieces into a cooking pot. To everyone's amazement, a young lamb emerged. Pelias was most impressed. This was his chance to be young again! On his urging, his three daughters killed him, chopped up his body, and threw the pieces in the bubbling cauldron. Of course, it was all a trick. The evil Pelias was dead at last.

Are you sure this will work, Medea?

Don't you trust me?

Jason flees

Jason never became king of Iolcus. He was forced to flee by Acastus, son of Pelias, who became the new king. Jason and Medea went to Corinth, where they settled down and had a family.

Happily ever after?

Medea and Jason had a fight, and she went away. Jason, who was lonely, visited the *Argo* to remember the good times. One day, the old ship's figurehead fell on Jason and killed him.

Father!

Ask the storyteller

What happened to the Golden Fleece?

Before he settled in Corinth, Jason took the Golden Fleece to the temple of Zeus at Orchomenus, a city in eastern Greece, and that was where he left it.

Glossary

Birthright Possessions or titles that people have when they are born or because they are firstborn.

Centaur A mythical creature that was half-man, half-horse.

Channel A narrow stretch of water between two landmasses.

Cunning Trickery and intelligence.

Epic A long poem about war and the deeds of heroes.

Figurehead The decorative statue attached to the front of a ship.

Harpies Flying creatures with bird-like bodies and women's heads, known for snatching children.

Inherit To receive wealth or a title from someone when he or she dies.

Invincible Unable to be harmed.

Lyre A stringed musical instrument popular in ancient Greece.

Mortal A being who will die one day or who can be killed.

Oracle A person who can tell what will happen in the future.

Pilgrim Someone on a religious journey.

Prophecy A tale of what will happen in the future.

Sacrifice To kill an animal and offer it to the gods.

Siren A creature that is part-bird, part-woman, whose beautiful singing lured sailors to their doom on the rocky coast.

Soothsayer A person who uses observations of nature to predict the future.

Temple A place of worship. Most gods had temples built in their honor.

Who's Who

Acastus (a-CASS-tus) Son of Pelias.

Aeetes (ah-EE-tees) King of Colchis, owner of the Golden Fleece.

Aello (ELL-o) A harpy whose name means "Storm."

Aeson (EE-son) Father of Jason and half-brother of Pelias.

Alcimede (al-SIM-ih-dee) Mother of Jason.

Apsyrtus (ap-SUR-tus) Brother of Medea.

Argus (AR-guss) Argonaut; builder of the *Argo*.

Athena (uh-THEE-na) Goddess of war.

Butes (BYOO-teez) Argonaut lured by the sirens' singing.

Cadmus (CAD-muhs) Hero who killed a dragon that had magical teeth.

Calais (KAL-ace) Winged Argonaut who chased the harpies away from Phineus.

Chiron (KYE-ron) Kindly centaur who raised the infant Jason.

Chrysomallus (kriss-o-MALL-us) The flying, talking ram with a fleece of gold.

Cretheus (KRET-ee-us) Founder of Iolcus; father of Aeson and Pelias; grandfather of Jason.

Cyzicus (SIZ-ih-kuss) King of Cyzicus who was acidentally killed by Jason.

Hera (HEE-ra) Wife of Zeus; queen of the gods.

Hercules (HER-cue-leez) A Greek hero with great strength.

Idmon (ID-mon) Argonaut who could forecast the future.

Jason (JAY-sun) Commander of the Argo; leader of the expedition to capture the Golden Fleece.

Medea (med-EE-ah) Wife of Jason; daughter of King Aeetes.

Ocypete (oss-IP-ee-tee) A harpy whose name means "Swift Flier."

Orpheus (OR-fee-us) Argonaut who was a great poet and singer.

Pelias (PELL-ee-ass) Half-brother of Aeson; unlawful king of Iolcus.

Phineus (FIN-ee-us) Blind king who could see the future.

Talos (TAL-us) A bronze giant killed by the Argonauts at Crete.

Zetes (ZEE-teez) Winged Argonaut who chased the harpies away from Phineus.

Zeus (ZOOS) King of the gods.

Index